A LIFEGUIDE®  BIBLE STUDY

A N G E L S

*12 Studies
for individuals or groups*

Douglas Connelly

With Notes for Leaders

InterVarsity Press
Downers Grove, Illinois

InterVarsity Press® is the book-publishing division of InterVarsity Christian Fellowship®, a student movement active on campus at hundreds of universities, colleges and schools of nursing in the United States of America, and a member movement of the International Fellowship of Evangelical Students. For information about local and regional activities, write Public Relations Dept., InterVarsity Christian Fellowship, 6400 Schroeder Rd., P.O. Box 7895, Madison, WI 53707-7895.

All Scripture quotations, unless otherwise indicated, are taken from the HOLY BIBLE, NEW INTERNATIONAL VERSION®. NIV®. Copyright ©1973, 1978, 1984 by International Bible Society. Used by permission of Zondervan Publishing House. All rights reserved.

Some material in the introductions and notes was originally published in Angels Around Us by Douglas Connelly © 1994.

Cover photograph: Dennis Frates

ISBN 0-8308-1074-9

Printed in the United States of America ∞

22	21	20	19	18	17	16	15	14	13	12	11	10	9	8	7	6
13	12	11	10	09	08	07	06	05	04	03	02	01	00			

Contents

Getting the Most
from LifeGuide® Bible Studies

Many of us long to fill our minds and our lives with Scripture. We desire to be transformed by its message. LifeGuide® Bible Studies are designed to be an exciting and challenging way to do just that. They help us to be guided by God's Word in every area of life.

How They Work

LifeGuides have a number of distinctive features. Perhaps the most important is that they are *inductive* rather than *deductive*. In other words, they lead us to *discover* what the Bible says rather than simply *telling* us what it says.

They are also thought-provoking. They help us to think about the meaning of the passage so that we can truly understand what the author is saying. The questions require more than one-word answers.

The studies are personal. Questions expose us to the promises, assurances, exhortations and challenges of God's Word. They are designed to allow the Scriptures to renew our minds so that we can be transformed by the Spirit of God. This is the ultimate goal of all Bible study.

The studies are versatile. They are designed for student, neighborhood and church groups. They are also effective for individual study.

How They're Put Together

LifeGuides also have a distinctive format. Each study need take no more than forty-five minutes in a group setting or thirty minutes in personal study—unless you choose to take more time.

The studies can be used within a quarter system in a church and fit well in a semester or trimester system on a college campus. If a guide has more than thirteen studies, it is divided into two or occasionally three parts of approximately twelve studies each.

LifeGuides use a workbook format. Space is provided for writing answers to each question. This is ideal for personal study and allows group members to prepare in advance for the discussion.

The studies also contain leader's notes. They show how to lead a group discussion, provide additional background information on certain questions, give helpful tips on group dynamics and suggest ways to deal with problems which may arise during the discussion. With such helps, someone with little or no experience can lead an effective study.

Suggestions for Individual Study

1. As you begin each study, pray that God will help you to understand and apply the passage to your life.

2. Read and reread the assigned Bible passage to familiarize yourself with what the author is saying. In the case of book studies, you may want to read through the entire book prior to the first study. This will give you a helpful overview of its contents.

3. A good modern translation of the Bible, rather than the King James Version or a paraphrase, will give you the most help. The New International Version, the New American Standard Bible and the Revised Standard Version are all recommended. However, the questions in this guide are based on the New International Version.

4. Write your answers in the space provided in the study guide. This will help you to express your understanding of the passage clearly.

5. It might be good to have a Bible dictionary handy. Use it to look up any unfamiliar words, names or places.

Suggestions for Group Study

1. Come to the study prepared. Follow the suggestions for individual study mentioned above. You will find that careful preparation will greatly enrich your time spent in group discussion.

2. Be willing to participate in the discussion. The leader of your group will not be lecturing. Instead, he or she will be encouraging the members of the group to discuss what they have learned from the passage. The leader will be asking the questions that are found in this guide. Plan to share what God has taught you in your individual study.

3. Stick to the passage being studied. Your answers should be based on the verses which are the focus of the discussion and not on outside authorities such as commentaries or speakers. This guide deliberately avoids jumping from book to book or passage to passage. Each study focuses on only one

passage. Book studies are generally designed to lead you through the book in the order in which it was written. This will help you follow the author's argument.

4. Be sensitive to the other members of the group. Listen attentively when they share what they have learned. You may be surprised by their insights! Link what you say to the comments of others so the group stays on the topic. Also, be affirming whenever you can. This will encourage some of the more hesitant members of the group to participate.

5. Be careful not to dominate the discussion. We are sometimes so eager to share what we have learned that we leave too little opportunity for others to respond. By all means participate! But allow others to also.

6. Expect God to teach you through the passage being discussed and through the other members of the group. Pray that you will have an enjoyable and profitable time together.

7. If you are the discussion leader, you will find additional suggestions and helpful ideas for each study in the leader's notes. These are found at the back of the guide.

Introducing Angels

In the unseen realms of God's universe, powerful and wonderful beings dwell. They move at the speed of light to carry out their master's will. They are involved in the political affairs of nations and in the smallest concerns of children. They may stand guard over your life and protect you in countless ways. They watch what goes on in the church where you worship and they engage in cosmic battles that you aren't even aware of. These fantastic beings are called angels.

Angels are a hot commodity! You can find dozens of books on angels in most bookstores. The newspapers of cities large and small announce seminars taught by people who promise to "put you in touch with your angel." Even the major news magazines have devoted front cover stories to the rising interest in angels.

Unfortunately, many Christians have believed a lot of very bad information about angels from some very misguided sources. A friend of mine who manages a Christian bookstore told me that several Christian people have come in asking for a book on how to pray to your angel or on how to learn your guardian angel's name. Most of the books claiming to tell us the truth about angels have turned to every source of information except the genuine source of truth—God's Word. Angel lore, myths, ancient stories, even the experiences of people who have encountered angels must be measured against the standard of God's truth. I've written this study guide to help you discover for yourself what the Bible says about these marvelous beings.

And when you go to the Bible, you won't be disappointed! Thirty-four of the Bible's sixty-six books talk about angels in detail. Every New Testament writer confirms their existence. The word *angel* occurs more than 250 times in Scripture. This is certainly no isolated truth hidden in the dark corners of the Bible! Jesus himself referred to angels as real beings who were involved in every realm of human activity. So if you have thought that angels belong in the same category as sea monsters and trolls, think again.

The Bible also makes it clear that angels fall into two distinct groups—the holy angels of God and the evil angels who followed Satan in his rebellion. Most New Age angel guides ignore that aspect of God's truth. What they don't tell you is that the angel you "get in touch with" may destroy you. The best protection we have against the deception of Satan is a firm knowledge of God's Word. Our example is the Lord Jesus, who, when tempted by the Enemy, rebuked him with the powerful living Word of the living God.

To get at the wealth of information the Bible has about angels, this guide has a unique format. As with other LifeGuides, each study focuses on one key Scripture passage. That passage will be the primary source of our study and discussion. At the end of each study, however, you will find an additional section called "Expanding Your Perspective." In it you will be directed to one or two other related passages that will deepen your understanding of a particular aspect of the nature or work of angels. If you are studying with a group, you can cover these sections in the group at the end of the study or on your own either before or after the study.

We are about to embark on an exciting adventure. You will be reminded of things you have learned before, and (hopefully) you will learn some new truths too. My desire is that you will be open as never before to understanding and enjoying the wonderful ministry that God's angels have in your life.

1
Burning in God's Presence

Isaiah 6:1-8

During a particularly difficult year of my life, I experienced some profound and wonderful times of worship. Usually these came as my wife and I visited a church in our community for their midweek service. The believers began with an extended time of singing praises to the Lord. A period of prayer followed. I often sat through the whole service in tears of brokenness before God. I left in awe of the glory of God and with a transforming sense of his cleansing in my life.

The prophet Isaiah must have come to the Lord's temple with the same sense of longing for God's presence and power. What he saw as he came in worship was a stunning vision not only of the Lord, but also of magnificent angels who shouted God's praise.

1. Describe a time when you had a sense of God's close presence and glory. Where were you, and what feelings did you experience?

2. Read Isaiah 6:1-8. What circumstances and personal struggles might have

burdened Isaiah's heart as he came into the temple?

3. Imagine yourself in Isaiah's place. What would you tell a friend that you saw, felt, heard and smelled in verses 1-4?

4. Why does Isaiah have such a strong reaction to his experience (v. 5)?

5. The angel beings Isaiah saw above God's throne are called *seraphs*. The word means "burning ones." Why do you think they would be portrayed as burning?

6. Based on Isaiah's description of the appearance, words and actions of the seraphs, what conclusions can you draw about their character?

7. How would you summarize the mission of the seraphs?

8. How do you think Isaiah felt as he left the temple?

9. How do you think Isaiah's personal worship was affected by this vision?

10. How will Isaiah's vision make a difference in your worship of God? (For example, does the fact that holy angels are worshiping with you give you greater confidence or make you more reluctant?)

11. What are some appropriate ways that we can acknowledge the presence of angels in our corporate worship services?

Expanding Your Perspective

12. Read Revelation 5:11-12. In John's vision of heaven, millions of angels surround God's throne. What seem to be their primary functions?

13. You may want to conclude this study with a time of personal or group worship before the Lord. Choose one or more of the many worship hymns based on either Isaiah 6 or Revelation 5—for example, "Holy, Holy, Holy" (Heber/Dykes), "Holy, Holy" (Owen) and "Worthy Is the Lamb" (Wyrtzen). As you worship, picture the angels of God worshiping with you. Your voices and praises join together to exalt the Lord!

2
Angels Among Us
Genesis 18:1-22; 19:1-29

Esther Maas, or Aunt Et, as she is known to dozens of missionary kids around the world, was on her way to church on April 13, 1988. A short distance from home she was involved in a car accident. Almost immediately a man appeared at her van door. He took Esther's hand, and at his touch a comforting peace spread over her. The man was in his thirties, he wore tan work clothes and needed a shave. He asked one bystander to go to a nearby store and call 911. When Esther asked his name, he said he couldn't tell her his name but that she would be fine. The man stayed until the emergency crew arrived and then was gone. No one got his name, and except for this saint of God who needed comfort and care, no one remembered much about him.

When Esther related the story to Christian friends, several of them immediately concluded that an angel had helped her. This man may not have been an angel, of course, but his ministry certainly falls in line with what we know from Scripture as angelic care.

---

1. Imagine that you are responsible to hire a personal guardian angel. What job requirements would you list in the help-wanted ad?

2. Read Genesis 18:1-22. What facts from the text demonstrate that the three men who visited Abraham appeared to be three normal human travelers (18:3-5)?

_____

3. What evidence can you find in the passage that at least one of these men was a supernatural being?

_____

4. Do you think Abraham sensed that they were not just ordinary travelers? Explain your answer.

_____

5. Read Genesis 19:1-29. Two of the men who visited Abraham are now specifically identified as "angels" (19:1), yet they still appear very much like human men. List the supernatural actions of these two angels.

What can you learn from their actions about the power of angels?

_____

6. Do you think Lot knew that these men were angels? Explain your answer.

_____

7. What do you think would have happened to the two angels if Lot had not taken them in?

What would have happened to Lot if he had refused to welcome them?

---

8. In God's dealings with Abraham, Lot and the city of Sodom, how do the angels demonstrate God's judgment and God's mercy?

---

9. With whom in this story do you most closely identify and why—interceding Abraham, hesitant Lot (19:16), the rescuing angels, the mocking sons-in-law (19:14) or Lot's disobedient wife (19:17, 26)?

---

10. What do these verses reveal to you about how you may experience angels?

---

11. How receptive are you to the intervention of angels in your life? Explain.

Expanding Your Perspective
12. Read Hebrews 13:2. Should we expect to encounter angels, or is this an experience limited to only a few? Explain your answer.

---

13. What specific actions can you take to implement this command to "entertain strangers" more fully into your life?

3
The Angel of the Lord
Judges 13

A remarkable person flashes across the pages of the Old Testament. He is called "the angel of the Lord." On several occasions at crisis times for God's people, this amazing being appears. He speaks with incredible authority. He acts with startling power. Sometimes he brings severe judgment; sometimes he brings gentle comfort. He leaves those who see him in awe.

On one very ordinary day in the time of the judges in Israel, one very ordinary couple had a visit from the angel of the Lord. They were certain of one thing when he left—he was no ordinary angel!

1. Describe a time when you or a friend of yours doubted some promise of God's. How was that doubt resolved?

2. Read Judges 13. Based on the wife's testimony (vv. 3-7), describe the angel of the Lord.

3. Compare and contrast the reactions of Manoah and his wife to the first visit from the angel (vv. 1-8).

_____

4. Why did Manoah pray that God would send the angel back (v. 8)?

_____

5. Which of the restrictions that the angel placed on Manoah's wife and yet-to-be-born son would you find most difficult and why?

_____

6. In what specific ways have you separated yourself unto God?

_____

7. In verse 16 we are told that Manoah did not realize it was an angel of the Lord. Then verse 22 tells us Manoah believed that they had seen God. What was it about the appearance or the actions of the angel of the Lord that might have led Manoah to that conclusion?

_____

8. Which person seems to have better spiritual insight—Manoah or his wife? Why do you think that is the case?

_____

9. When are you most likely to question God or his promises?

10. What insights have you gained from this study that will help you to resolve your doubts?

Expanding Your Perspective
11. The same angel of the Lord appeared unexpectedly to Moses in the burning bush. Read Exodus 3:1-6. What confirmation do you find in this account that the angel of the Lord was in fact a visible appearance of God?

_____

12. If this wonderful being was deity, why is he called an *angel?*

_____

13. Read Psalm 34:4-7. What does this promise about "the angel of the Lord" convey to you about the care and protection of the Lord for you as an individual?

_____

14. How has the Lord recently demonstrated his personal care for you?

4
Jesus and the Angels
Hebrews 1

O ur son, Kyle, loves zoos! We plan our trips and vacations around the
zoos and animal parks we haven't visited yet. One day as we walked to the
entrance of a new zoo, I said teasingly, "Kyle, what if one of the zookeepers
wants to put you in a cage?"

"No, he won't do that," Kyle responded.

"Why not?" I asked.

"Because, Dad," came the exasperated answer, "I'm a *people!*"

Our four-year-old had grasped the essential, God-given difference between animals and human beings.

Some people in the early decades of the New Testament were having a
struggle with the difference between Jesus and the angels of God. The angels
had given the law of God to Moses on Mount Sinai. The angels were powerful,
awesome beings. Jesus, these people said, was a great prophet, even a great
angel, but not God. The writer of the book of Hebrews determined to set
the record straight once and for all. As wonderful as angels are, they can't
compare with Jesus.

---

1. If you were asked, "Who is Jesus Christ?" how would you respond?

2. Read Hebrews 1. What facts about Jesus are declared in verses 1-3?

3. Verses 4-5 discuss Christ's name. Several times in the Old Testament angels are called "sons of God" (see Job 1:6; 2:1 NASB). But no angel was ever given the title "Son." What is the distinction between the two titles?

4. What contrast does the writer draw between angels in verse 7 and the Son in verse 8?

5. What do the images of wind and flames of fire (v. 7) convey to you about the character and work of angels?

6. The writer of Hebrews paints a powerful portrait of Jesus as the sovereign King of the universe. How does that portrait bring encouragement to you in your present circumstances?

7. What aspects of God's character are emphasized in verses 10-12?

8. How would you describe the place angels hold in God's eternal plan as compared to the place Christ holds?

9. The angels (in contrast to Christ) are called God's "ministering servants sent to serve those who will inherit salvation." In what ways does that fact encourage you?

---

10. Since angels do serve us, why would it be wrong to pray to an angel for assistance in a crisis?

Expanding Your Perspective
11. Even though Jesus was superior to the angels, several times during his ministry angels ministered to him. Read Mark 1:12-13. What specific things could angels have done in this situation to help and encourage Jesus?

---

12. An angel also came to Jesus' aid near the end of his earthly ministry. Read Luke 22:39-44. How do you think an angel could have strengthened Jesus as he faced the cross?

---

13. Based on what you have learned from this study, what are some ways that holy angels might be serving or ministering to you that you have been unaware of?

5
Lower Than the Angels
Hebrews 2:5-18

A friend of mine was the leader of an engineering division within one of the Big Three automakers. Because of restructuring within the company, he found himself in a different unit at the bottom of the engineering ladder. The change put my friend's character to the test, but he handled the transition well. It takes a lot of humility to handle a change like that gracefully.

From eternity Jesus had existed as God. But, in order to identify with us and in order to redeem us, Jesus became fully human. In the realm of his humanity, the Lord of the angels lived for thirty-three years as a man, lower than the very beings he had created.

1. Describe a time when you had to carry out some demeaning task. How did you feel?

2. Read Hebrews 2:5-18. According to verses 5-8, what place of honor did God give to human beings in his original plan?

3. If God's original intention was to give humanity dominion over the created world, what caused the delay in that plan? (Note verse 8: "Yet *at present* we do not see everything subject to him [that is, subject to humanity].")

4. In what respects was Jesus made "a little lower than the angels"?

5. Jesus fulfilled God's original intention for human beings. What benefits come to believers because Jesus as a human being is "now crowned with glory and honor" (v. 9)?

6. Christians often are called upon to defend the deity of Jesus. Why is it just as important to believe in and to defend the full humanity of Jesus?

7. One result of Jesus' death, according to verse 14, was that Jesus "might destroy him who holds the power of death—that is, the devil." Why do we still struggle with the devil if Jesus died to destroy him?

8. In what ways is humanity held in slavery by fear of death (v. 15)?

9. Why does verse 16 emphasize that Jesus helps humans and not angels?

10. In what ways did Jesus' experience as a human being prepare him for his present ministry to us (vv. 17-18)?

11. How has this study changed your view of yourself as a human being?

Expanding Your Perspective
12. Read 1 Corinthians 6:1-3. As human beings we are lower than angels in glory and power now. What hint are we given in this passage that someday we will be exalted above angels?

13. How do you feel in the face of this responsibility?

How does what you have learned about the character and example of Jesus help you to face this awesome task?

6
Our Ancient Foe

Isaiah 14:3-15

Ｏne startling fact the Bible reveals about angels is that Satan, the most evil and powerful enemy of God and God's people, was once a beautiful and holy angel. He was called "the son of the dawn" and occupied a place of honor near God's throne. But pride and desire began to develop in the heart of this glorious angel. He thought that because he dwelled so near to God that he could become like God.

Satan's rebellious rise and stunning collapse are described for us in poetic drama by the prophet Isaiah. What begins as a taunt against the evil human king of Babylon soon becomes a taunt against the real power behind Babylon's throne, Satan himself.

---

1. What are your fears or concerns as you begin a study of our evil enemy, Satan?

Spend some time in prayer asking God to protect your heart and mind as you focus on Satan and his power.

2. Read Isaiah 14:3-15. In verses 3-11 Isaiah describes the death of the future human king of Babylon who would bring the people of Israel into cruel bondage. What can you learn about the character of this man from the prophetic description of his end?

3. What will life without this king be like (vv. 3, 7-9)?

4. What changes do you see in verses 12-15 that would lead you to believe that a different being is addressed in those verses—a supernatural being rather than a mere human being?

5. Five times "the son of the dawn" is said to proclaim, "I will." Explain how each claim is a direct assault on the character or plan of God (vv. 13-14).

6. What do these claims tell you about the character and power of this being?

7. In what ways is Satan still trying to make himself "like the Most High" (v. 14)?

8. How do you see Satan's rebellious attitude reflected in contemporary culture?

9. What perspective does this passage give you on God's attitude toward a proud person who tries to be like God?

10. In what situations do you find yourself trying to try to take control of what should be under God's control?

Expanding Your Perspective
11. Read Revelation 12:7-10 and 1 Peter 5:8. From these two passages, how would you characterize Satan's actions toward believers?

12. Read 1 Peter 5:9 and James 4:7. In what practical ways can you resist the devil's attacks and accusations in your life?

13. What promises can you claim from these verses when you stand against Satan?

7
Dealing with Demons
Mark 5:1-20

I had never had a direct confrontation with one of Satan's angels, but the man standing in front of me was definitely under demonic control. He had come into our church on a Sunday morning, but he had not come as a worshiper. A look of disdain for everything we stood for was in his eyes—and there was something more. The power of evil surrounded him. I sensed it the moment I came near him. As I walked to the front of the auditorium to begin the service, I asked the Spirit of God to block the influence of any evil spirits upon our worship. The power of God's Spirit was evident that morning as the congregation worshiped with joy and listened to God's Word with intense interest.

When Satan rebelled against the Lord and was cast down from his exalted position, a large group of angels followed him. These angels are actively pursuing Satan's agenda. Modern psychologists and even some theologians want to dismiss demons as an ancient myth. Jesus, however, believed that demons were real. He battled with them dozens of times.

---

1. Do you believe you have ever encountered a demon or demonic power? Explain.

2. Read Mark 5:1-20. How would you feel if you lived near the man described in verses 1-5?

3. When Jesus addresses the man in verses 6-9, who responds—the man or the demons? Explain.

4. What can you learn from this account of the power of demons over a person who is totally possessed or controlled by an evil spirit?

What can you conclude about the physical, emotional and spiritual oppression that people under demonic influence experience?

5. The demons recognized Jesus immediately even though Jesus had never been in the region of the Gerasenes. What does that tell you about the knowledge of fallen angels?

6. Is it possible for people to be controlled by demons to the same degree today? Explain.

If it is possible, how would the presence of the demons be revealed in our culture?

7. How would you evaluate the response of the people living in the area to

Jesus' restoration of the man (vv. 14-20)?

8. What steps can we as Christians take to help someone who is oppressed by demonic forces?

What risks are involved in confronting demonic powers?

9. In your opinion can a genuine Christian be possessed like the man in this passage was? Explain to what level you believe a Christian can be "demonized."

10. Is there an area of your life in which you feel evil influences are trying to gain control? If so, how are you fighting against these influences?

What specific steps can you take to keep your spiritual life and focus in balance?

Expanding Your Perspective
11. Read Luke 13:10-17. What do you think were the real reasons for the synagogue ruler's indignant reaction to this deliverance?

12. Based on these two incidents in Jesus' ministry, what should our response be to a person's genuine deliverance and restoration from demonic oppression?

8
The Battle Against Us
Ephesians 6:10-20

I guess it finally had to come to this—Bible trading cards! The bookstore display was designed to catch the eye of any fourteen-year-old. Three different sets of cards were available. (Sorry, no bubble gum.) I expected the cards of Old Testament heroes and New Testament apostles, but the third set was the most intriguing. It was called "Spiritual Warfare." The cover drawing was of a red-haired Satan tumbling out of heaven. The other cards showed holy angels and fallen angels battling each other or wrestling for influence over a human being.

What disturbed me about the cards was not what they portrayed. There is a spiritual battle raging in the angelic realm. Evil powers of darkness do seek to undermine us as believers. I was disturbed by the way that this very real spiritual battle was trivialized. The angels became comic book characters; the struggle was pushed into the realm of fantasy. But spiritual warfare is not a video game. It is part of every Christian's experience. If we ignore the forces arrayed against us, we are walking toward disaster.

---

1. How do you think the people you work with would respond if you tried to explain that you as a Christian are engaged in spiritual warfare?

2. Read Ephesians 6:10-20. Why does Paul stress that we are to "put on the full armor of God" (vv. 11, 13)?

3. Based particularly on verses 12, 13 and 16, how would you characterize the spiritual battle that we are in?

4. What evidence do you see of this spiritual struggle in your own life?

in your church?

in your nation?

5. Do you think every Christian is in the battle, or can a Christian choose to avoid the battle? Explain your answer.

6. Explain in your own words the meaning and importance of each piece of spiritual armor (vv. 14-17).
   Belt:
   Breastplate:
   Footwear:
   Shield:
   Helmet:
   Sword:

7. The word *schemes* in verse 11 implies a well-developed plan of attack. Where does Satan find it easiest to attack you?

8. Which piece of armor do you need to "put on" to defend yourself in your area of weakness, and what do you need to do to get that piece of armor ready for battle?

_____

9. Why is prayer so important in this battle (v. 18)?

_____

10. Paul did not hesitate to ask the Ephesian Christians to pray for specific things for him (vv. 19-20). What specific requests can you share with a trusted friend or the members of your study group that will help you be more victorious in your daily battles?

_____

Expanding Your Perspective
11. The imagery of the battle is only one description of the Christian life. It is also compared to a walk, a race, a rest and a challenging adventure. What happens to us if we see the Christian experience only as a battle?

_____

What happens to us if we ignore the fact that the Christian life involves spiritual warfare?

_____

12. The angels of God are often portrayed in Scripture as the Lord's host or army. Read 2 Kings 6:15-17. What feelings would you have experienced in this situation if you had seen what Elisha's servant saw?

_____

13. In what circumstances might we experience angel warriors fighting with us in spiritual battles?

9
Angels and Guidance
Acts 8:26-40; 10:1-48

The meeting had lasted several hours. Every aspect of the decision we were facing had been debated, analyzed and discussed. All that remained was to make the decision! A long silence settled over the room. An elder put everything in perspective with one question: "How do we know if this is God's will?"

That is a question every Christian faces at times. We would be willing to make any decision, even one that would result in difficulty and sacrifice, if we just knew for certain what God's will was.

Sometimes God gives his people guidance when they aren't even seeking it. The early Christians were pretty content to keep the gospel confined within the Jewish community. What burdened God's heart, however, was the world! So God began to move his people in a totally new and unexpected direction—and God used angels to help open the door.

---

1. Think back to a time when you needed the Lord's guidance in a decision. How did you seek out God's direction?

2. Read Acts 8:26-40. Describe both what the angel does and how Philip responds (vv. 26-28).

3. God sent an angel to point Philip in the direction of a seeking man. Why didn't God just send the angel directly to the eunuch?

4. An angel directed Philip to the road; the Spirit of God directed him to a specific man (v. 29). What distinctions can you draw between how an angel may guide a believer and how the Spirit guides a believer?

5. God obviously "sets up" this opportunity to witness about Christ. How does that perspective free you from fears about evangelism?

6. I wonder if most Christians would know their Bibles well enough to answer the eunuch's questions (vv. 31-35). What steps can you take to grow in knowledge and faith so you will be prepared for such opportunities?

7. Read Acts 10. How would you characterize Cornelius's responses to God's messages?

How would you characterize Peter's responses to the messages he received?

8. An angel brought God's message to Cornelius, but the Holy Spirit spoke to Peter (vv. 19-20). When you are seeking God's guidance, should you look for an angel, listen for the Spirit's voice, or both? Explain how you came to your conclusion.

9. If a friend told you that an angel had given him or her specific guidance in a decision, how would you respond to your friend's claim?

10. Peter's visit resulted in the conversion of Cornelius's whole family. Should we look for confirming evidence of God's leading in our lives? Why or why not?

Expanding Your Perspective
11. Read Matthew 1:20-21 and 2:13, 19-20. Three times an angel appeared to Joseph in a dream. What specific details would lead Joseph to conclude that these were genuine angelic messages and not just imaginative fantasies?

12. Would you rather have the permanent (but quiet) leading of the Spirit in your life or the occasional (but spectacular) instruction of angels? Explain your answer.

13. As the result of this study, what will you ask God for when you must make a difficult decision?

10
Guarded by Angels

Acts 12:1-17

Several years ago my mother visited a Christian friend of hers who was hospitalized in the intensive care unit. Her friend had been in a serious car accident and was not expected to live. When my mother came into the room one evening, her friend said, "Mary, I'm going to be okay. An angel has been sitting at the foot of my bed all day."

One of the most wonderful ministries of angels is their protective care over believers in Jesus Christ. Usually that care is exercised in quiet, almost unnoticeable ways, but sometimes it can be astonishing. The apostle Peter learned to appreciate the protection of angels—on his way out of a locked prison!

---

1. Describe a time when you or someone you know was protected from harm in a remarkable way.

---

2. Read Acts 12:1-17. What indications can you find in the text that Peter was calm even when he was under arrest?

3. What thoughts might have crossed Peter's mind when he was awakened by an angel (vv. 6-7)?

4. What do the angel's actions tell you about the nature and ministry of angels (vv. 6-11)?

5. Why did God send an angel—a personal being—to lead Peter out rather than just instantly removing him from the prison?

6. Men and women just as faithful to God as Peter have been arrested and have died in prison. God allowed James to be executed (v. 2) but rescued Peter. Why doesn't God *always* deliver his people?

7. Twice we are told that the Christians were praying for Peter (vv. 5 and 12). If a Christian is in danger or in trouble, should that Christian (or his Christian friends) ask God to send an angel for deliverance or protection? Explain your answer.

8. What strikes you as unusual about the response of the Christians who were praying when Peter appeared at the gate of Mary's house (vv. 12-17)?

How do you think Peter felt as he stood at the gate?

9. These Christians obviously were not expecting God to work like he did. In what ways do we "limit" God when we ask him to work in a particular situation?

Expanding Your Perspective

10. Psalm 91:9-13 is a general promise to God's people of angelic protection. Read that passage carefully. What statements in these verses indicate that you and I can claim these promises of angelic care even today?

11. Read Matthew 18:10. What conclusions can you draw about angelic care over children from Jesus' statement?

12. How should Jesus' warning shape our attitudes toward children?

13. Based on the passages you have studied, do you think that all Christians have guardian angels? Why or why not?

11
Discerning the Spirits
1 John 4:1-6

At the end of a seminar on angels, a woman came up to me and said that she had a wonderful angel story to tell me. It seems that this woman's best friend had a daughter who became seriously ill. The doctors were baffled about how to diagnose and treat her illness. One day as the little girl's mother was praying for God's help, she heard a weak scratching at her front door. She opened the door to find a small tabby kitten. The first thing she noticed, I was told, "was a white halo of fur around the kitten's ears." The kitten ran to the sick girl's room and jumped on the bed. The little girl was delighted and held the kitten close. Within two days the girl's symptoms had disappeared, and she was out of bed. On the third day, when the kitten was let outside in the morning, it never returned. The mother was convinced that the kitten was an angel who came to bring healing to her daughter.

As heartwarming as that story is, I have never repeated it as an account of a genuine angelic appearance. I haven't used it in that way for one simple reason. The story does not harmonize with what I read in the Bible about angels. In Scripture angels never appear to human beings as animals.

Evaluating the experiences of other people is difficult. We feel so judgmental. This chapter will help you see the vital importance of doing just that, however. To fully accept whatever you are told may be dangerous to your spiritual health!

---

1. On a scale of one to ten, with one referring to a complete skeptic and ten referring to someone who completely accepts what other people say, where would you rank yourself when it comes to believing the accounts people tell of extraordinary spiritual experiences? Why?

2. What are some of the results of being too closed-minded to new spiritual experiences or new insights?

What are the results of openly embracing any new teaching or experience that comes along?

3. Read 1 John 4:1-6. How would you characterize the Christians to whom John writes—too narrow-minded or too open-minded? Support your answer from these verses.

4. We are told to "test the spirits" because there are many false prophets (v. 1). What would be some examples of false prophets today?

5. What "test" does John put forth to use in determining whether a particular teaching is from God or not (vv. 2-3)?

6. John lists some other methods of recognizing falsehood in verses 4-6. Describe them.

7. What are some other practical tests that you can use to determine if a teaching or a person's experience is from God?

8. What encouragement to help us face false prophets does John give in verses 4-6?

9. Many Christians will justify a belief or an action by saying, "God told me," or "I prayed about it." In the light of these verses, is it sinful or judgmental to evaluate another Christian's experience by the standard of God's Word? Explain.

10. How should you respond to someone if his or her belief or experience contradicts the clear teaching of the Bible?

How should you respond if the person's belief or experience doesn't contradict Scripture but is different from your belief or experience?

Expanding Your Perspective
11. Read 2 Corinthians 11:13-15 and Galatians 1:8. In what ways might angels be involved in leading people away from the truth about Christ?

12. Imagine that your friend came to you and told you that he or she had received a message from an angel. How would you explain to that friend the importance of "testing" that experience according to God's Word?

13. What steps would you take to help your friend evaluate that angelic encounter?

12
God's Reapers
Matthew 13:24-50

Woman called me today to tell me about a book she had just read. The author had convinced her that Jesus was going to return before a certain date this year! She called with a conflicting sense of joy and panic—joy at the thought of Christ's soon return, and panic at the thought that members of her family would be left behind.

The Bible's predictions of the end of human history have encouraged and, at times, confused Christians for two thousand years. The *fact* that Christ will return and bring human rule to a crashing end is unquestioned. *When* that will happen is God's secret—and he hasn't let us in on it! We are to live every day in the light of Christ's coming. We do know, however, that when human history closes, angels will play a prominent part.

Jesus told a series of parables to his disciples one day. The parables seemed like harmless stories until Jesus explained their true meaning.

---

1. If you could ask Jesus one question about end times, what would you ask?

How do you think he would answer?

___

2. Read Matthew 13:24-30 and 36-43. Based on Jesus' explanation of the parable of the weeds in verses 37-43, identify the following characters or images in the parable:

The man who sowed the seed:

The good seed:

The enemy:

The bad seed:

The field:

The harvest:

The harvesters:

___

3. Describe the work of Jesus' angels at the end of the age when "the kingdom of [the] Father" is established (vv. 41-43).

___

4. Compare the end that awaits "the sons of the evil one" to what awaits "the sons of the kingdom."

___

5. How would you describe the spiritual "field" in which God has placed you?

___

6. Read Matthew 13:47-50. What differences and similarities can you find between the parable of the net (vv. 47-50) and the earlier parable of the weeds?

7. Why do you think angels are assigned the task of separating the good from the evil in both examples?

8. Which aspects of these two parable do you find most disturbing? Which aspects are most comforting?

9. What specific actions can you take to respond positively and obediently to what you have learned in these parables?

Expanding Your Perspective
10. Read Matthew 24:29-31. How is the work of God's angels in this passage different from their work depicted in the two parables?

11. Read 1 Thessalonians 4:15-18. Does the reality of Christ's return comfort you or threaten you? Explain your answer.

12. If you knew for certain that the Lord would return at a specific date this year, what changes would you make in your life?

What hinders you from making those changes right now?

13. We've come to the end of our study of these fascinating beings called angels. In what specific ways has this study changed your spiritual life?

Leader's Notes

Leading a Bible discussion can be an enjoyable and rewarding experience. But it can also be *scary*—especially if you've never done it before. If this is your feeling, you're in good company. When God asked Moses to lead the Israelites out of Egypt, he replied, "O Lord, please send someone else to do it!" (Ex 4:13).

When Solomon became king of Israel, he felt the task was beyond his abilities. "I am only a little child and do not know how to carry out my duties. . . . Who is able to govern this great people of yours?" (1 Kings 3:7, 9).

When God called Jeremiah to be a prophet, he replied, "Ah, Sovereign LORD, . . . I do not know how to speak; I am only a child" (Jer 1:6).

The list goes on. The apostles were "unschooled, ordinary men" (Acts 4:13). Timothy was young, frail and frightened. Paul's "thorn in the flesh" made him feel weak. But God's response to all of his servants—including you—is essentially the same: "My grace is sufficient for you" (2 Cor 12:9). Relax. God helped these people in spite of their weaknesses, and he can help you in spite of your feelings of inadequacy.

There is another reason why you should feel encouraged. Leading a Bible discussion is not difficult if you follow certain guidelines. You don't need to be an expert on the Bible or a trained teacher. The suggestions listed below should enable you to effectively and enjoyably fulfill your role as leader.

Preparing to Lead

1. Ask God to help you understand and apply the passage to your own life. Unless this happens, you will not be prepared to lead others. Pray too for the various members of the group. Ask God to give you an enjoyable and profitable time together studying his Word.

2. As you begin each study, read and reread the assigned Bible passage to familiarize yourself with what the author is saying. In the case of book studies, you may want to read through the entire book prior to the first study. This will give you a helpful overview of its contents.

3. This study guide is based on the New International Version of the Bible. It will help you and the group if you use this translation as the basis for your study and discussion. Encourage others to use the NIV also, but allow them the freedom to use whatever translation they prefer.

4. Carefully work through each question in the study. Spend time in meditation and reflection as you formulate your answers.

5. Write your answers in the space provided in the study guide. This will help you to express your understanding of the passage clearly.

6. It might help you to have a Bible dictionary handy. Use it to look up any unfamiliar words, names or places. (For additional help on how to study a passage, see chapter five of *Leading Bible Discussions,* IVP.)

7. Once you have finished your own study of the passage, familiarize yourself with the leader's notes for the study you are leading. These are designed to help you in several ways. First, they tell you the purpose the study guide author had in mind while writing the study. Take time to think through how the study questions work together to accomplish that purpose. Second, the notes provide you with additional background information or comments on some of the questions. This information can be useful if people have difficulty understanding or answering a question. Third, the leader's notes can alert you to potential problems you may encounter during the study.

8. If you wish to remind yourself of anything mentioned in the leader's notes, make a note to yourself below that question in the study.

Leading the Study

1. Begin the study on time. Unless you are leading an evangelistic Bible study, open with prayer, asking God to help you to understand and apply the passage.

2. Be sure that everyone in your group has a study guide. Encourage them to prepare beforehand for each discussion by working through the questions in the guide.

3. At the beginning of your first time together, explain that these studies are meant to be discussions not lectures. Encourage the members of the group to participate. However, do not put pressure on those who may be hesitant to speak during the first few sessions.

4. Read the introductory paragraph at the beginning of the discussion. This will orient the group to the passage being studied.

5. Read the passage aloud if you are studying one chapter or less. You may choose to do this yourself, or someone else may read if he or she has been asked to do so prior to the study. Longer passages may occasionally be read in parts at different times during the study. Some studies may cover several chapters. In such cases reading aloud would probably take too much time, so the group members should simply read the assigned passages prior to the study.

6. As you begin to ask the questions in the guide, keep several things in mind. First, the questions are designed to be used just as they are written. If you wish, you may simply read them aloud to the group. Or you may prefer to express them in your own words. However, unnecessary rewording of the questions is not recommended.

Second, the questions are intended to guide the group toward understanding and applying the *main idea* of the passage. The author of the guide has stated his or her view of this central idea in the *purpose* of the study in the leader's notes. You should try to understand how the passage expresses this idea and how the study questions work together to lead the group in that direction.

There may be times when it is appropriate to deviate from the study guide. For example, a question may have already been answered. If so, move on to the next question. Or someone may raise an important question not covered in the guide. Take time to discuss it! The important thing is to use discretion. There may be many routes you can travel to reach the goal of the study. But the easiest route is usually the one the author has suggested.

7. Avoid answering your own questions. If necessary, repeat or rephrase them until they are clearly understood. An eager group quickly becomes passive and silent if they think the leader will do most of the talking.

8. Don't be afraid of silence. People may need time to think about the question before formulating their answers.

9. Don't be content with just one answer. Ask, "What do the rest of you think?" or "Anything else?" until several people have given answers to the question.

10. Acknowledge all contributions. Try to be affirming whenever possible. Never reject an answer. If it is clearly wrong, ask, "Which verse led you to that conclusion?" or again, "What do the rest of you think?"

11. Don't expect every answer to be addressed to you, even though this will probably happen at first. As group members become more at ease, they will begin to truly interact with each other. This is one sign of a healthy discussion.

12. Don't be afraid of controversy. It can be very stimulating. If you don't resolve an issue completely, don't be frustrated. Move on and keep it in mind for later. A subsequent study may solve the problem.

13. Stick to the passage under consideration. It should be the source for answering the questions. Discourage the group from unnecessary cross-referencing. Likewise, stick to the subject and avoid going off on tangents.

14. Periodically summarize what the *group* has said about the passage. This helps to draw together the various ideas mentioned and gives continuity to the study. But don't preach.

15. Conclude your time together with conversational prayer. Be sure to ask God's help to apply those things which you learned in the study.

16. End on time.

Many more suggestions and helps are found in *Leading Bible Discussions* (IVP). Reading and studying through that would be well worth your time.

Components of Small Groups

A healthy small group should do more than study the Bible. There are four components you should consider as you structure your time together.

Nurture. Being a part of a small group should be a nurturing and edifying experience. You should grow in your knowledge and love of God and each other. If we are to properly love God, we must know and keep his commandments (Jn 14:15). That is why Bible study should be a foundational part of your small group. But you can be nurtured by other things as well. You can memorize Scripture, read and discuss a book, or occasionally listen to a tape of a good speaker.

Community. Most people have a need for close friendships. Your small group can be an excellent place to cultivate such relationships. Allow time for informal interaction before and after the study. Have a time of sharing during the meeting. Do fun things together as a group, such as a potluck supper or a picnic. Have someone bring refreshments to the meeting. Be creative!

Worship. A portion of your time together can be spent in worship and prayer. Praise God together for who he is. Thank him for what he has done and is doing in your lives and in the world. Pray for each other's needs. Ask God to help you to apply what you have learned. Sing hymns together.

Mission. Many small groups decide to work together in some form of outreach. This can be a practical way of applying what you have learned. You can host a series of evangelistic discussions for your friends or neighbors. You can visit people at a home for the elderly. Help a widow with cleaning or repair jobs around her home. Such projects can have a transforming influence on your group.

For a detailed discussion of the nature and function of small groups, read *Small Group Leaders' Handbook* or *Good Things Come in Small Groups* (both from IVP).

Study 1. Burning in God's Presence. Isaiah 6:1-8.

Purpose: To introduce the primary function of angels as the servants of God.

It might be helpful for you as the leader to prepare for this study by reading a biblical survey of the ministry of angels. Not every book—not even every Christian book—on angels can be trusted. Always compare what is taught with the teachings of Scripture.

In addition to my book *Angels Around Us* (Downers Grove, Ill.: InterVarsity Press, 1994), I would recommend C. Fred Dickason, *Angels: Elect and Evil* (Chicago: Moody Press, 1975) for a summary of the biblical teaching on angels.

As a leader you will have to exercise particular care throughout this study to evaluate the personal experiences of individuals. Many people believe they have had an encounter with an angel and have told their stories in widely read books or on talk shows. These experiences need to be compared carefully with the teachings of the Bible. I have included a chapter on "Evaluating Angel Encounters" in my book *Angels Around Us,* which may prove helpful.

Two key principles will guide you. First, it is not wrong or unspiritual to lovingly evaluate the experiences of another person, even of another Christian. The apostle John commanded us to "test the spirits," not to trust the spirits. Second, the key to evaluating another person's or even our own experiences is the Word of God. Measure what a person says about an angel encounter against God's truth. Whatever is in harmony with what we find in Scripture, we can accept. Whatever contradicts the teaching or the spirit of the Scriptures must be questioned or rejected. Your responsibility as the discussion leader will be to return the group to the clear teaching of the Bible as the only reliable source of truth in the realm of angels.

Question 1. Every study begins with an "approach" question, which is meant to be asked before the passage is read. These questions are important for several reasons.

First, they help the group to warm up to each other. No matter how well a group may know each other, there is always a stiffness that needs to be overcome before people will begin to talk openly. A good question will break the ice.

Second, approach questions get people thinking along the lines of the topic of the study. Most people will have lots of different things going on in their minds (dinner, an important meeting coming up, how to get the car fixed) that will have nothing to do with the study. A creative question will get their attention and draw them into the discussion.

Third, approach questions can reveal where our thoughts or feelings need to be transformed by Scripture. That is why it is especially important not to read the passage before the approach question is asked. The passage will tend to color the honest reactions people would otherwise give because they are, of course, supposed to think the way the Bible does. Giving honest responses before they find out what the Bible says may help them see where their thoughts or attitudes need to be changed.

Question 2. Isaiah's vision of the Lord came after the death of the godly king Uzziah in 740 B.C. Uzziah had ruled in righteous obedience until, in an act of pride, he tried to take the place of the priests by burning incense in the temple. He was struck with leprosy and lived as an outcast until his death (2 Chron 26:16-21). Uzziah is also called Azariah (2 Kings 14:21). Uzziah's death may have left Isaiah in a state of uncertainty about the nation's future and even his own future. He came to God's earthly temple seeking comfort and was given a vision of the sovereign King sitting in the heavenly temple.

Question 5. Early church theologians wrestled for a long time over the exact ranking and order of the angels. Thomas Aquinas finally settled on a nine-level hierarchy. According to his scheme, the seraphs were the highest and most powerful angels, who dwelt closest to the presence of God. They "burned" with God's holy brilliance!

You will often see these angels referred to as *seraphim*. In the Hebrew language, adding -*im* to a word makes it plural in form.

Question 6. It is important to emphasize that these angelic beings are personal beings. They have intelligence (to see and to respond to God's glory); they have a will (to act obediently to God's direction); they have the ability to speak (in praise to God and in communication with Isaiah). God created the angels as unique, personal beings who are able to relate to the other category of created personal beings—human beings—and to God (who is also a person).

Question 7. The primary functions of the seraphs are to stand or fly above God's throne and to continually declare God's holiness. They exist simply to attribute worth to God by announcing the perfection of his character. These powerful, majestic beings are perfectly fulfilled doing nothing other than worshiping the eternal God! The seraphs also (at least in Isaiah's case) became agents of God's purifying power as one of the seraphs touched Isaiah's lips with a burning coal in an act of consecration.

Question 10. We as believers should recognize that when we worship God either individually or corporately, we are not alone. Angels worship continually before God's throne.

Question 11. The angels are very interested in our corporate services and in the work of the local church. See, for example, 1 Timothy 5:21 and 1 Corinthians

11:10. Some suggestions for acknowledging the presence of angels are (1) to use Scripture readings or affirmations of faith which include references to God's angels, (2) to select hymns which point out the fact that angels are present with us to worship God or (3) to teach passages of Scripture that declare the truth about angels. Angels are never to be worshiped, but are worshipers with us of the true and living God.

Question 12. John is ushered into God's throne room at a crucial point in the history of our redemption. Millions of angels are gathered to see the beginning of God's final work of reclaiming his creation. These angels focus on worship and praise. They express verbally the wonders of God's character. That is exactly what worship is, whether it comes from a human believer or from an angel servant.

Question 13. The idea here is to praise God along with the angels. The recent rise in the popularity of angels has led some people to unbiblical extremes. We are never to worship or to pray to angels. Holy angels are pictured in the Bible as servants of God; they come to our aid at God's command, not because we call them (see Ps 103:20).

Study 2. Angels Among Us. Genesis 18:1-22; 19:1-29.

Purpose: To discover how angels appear to human beings in the Bible, and to consider whether that is still a possibility today.

Question 2. Some key indicators that these men appeared to be normal human beings may have been overlooked when you first read the passage. The travelers had feet that could be washed (18:4); they ate human food (18:5); they spoke human language (18:5). Apparently no angel wings were folded under their robes!

Question 3. One of the "men" who visited Abraham is called "the LORD" (18:1, 10, 13, 17, 20, 22). He also displayed attributes of deity. He knew what Sarah did and thought in secret (18:13); he claimed divine power (18:14); he was able to predict the future with certainty (18:14).

Question 6. Lot's offer of his daughters to the men of Sodom was certainly not an action of which the Lord (or the angels) approved. Lot realized the importance of protecting his guests, but he spoke out of desperation. The angels protected both Lot and his daughters. Lot's tendency to act foolishly in a crisis was picked up by the daughters, who later seduced their own father (Gen 19:30-38).

Question 8. The rescue of Lot and the destruction of Sodom became a common illustration of God's ability to rescue the righteous and to punish the wicked. See 2 Peter 2:6-9 and Jude 7; also Deuteronomy 29:23; Isaiah

1:9; 13:19; Jeremiah 50:40; Amos 4:11.

Question 9. Lot's wife became a proverbial warning to later generations (see Lk 17:32). Even today, large, weirdly shaped salt formations at the southern end of the Dead Sea are reminders of her desire to cling to the old lifestyle even as it was in the process of being destroyed.

Question 12. Some Bible scholars believe that the writer of Hebrews was referring back to Abraham and Lot and their angelic visitors and not to the possibility of angels visiting believers today. That interpretation in my mind is too limited. As I read the passage, the writer clearly opens the door to the possibility that angels may at times enter into this realm for our blessing. Keep in mind, however, that direct angelic encounters are rare in the biblical narrative. Not every Christian will have a visit from an angel.

Study 3. The Angel of the Lord. Judges 13.

Purpose: To help us understand and identify the Old Testament person, the angel of the Lord, and his ministry in our lives.

Question 2. You may want to read the main accounts of the appearances of the angel of the Lord to get a clearer view of his character and power. He appeared to Hagar (Gen 16:7-14), Jacob (Gen 32:22-32; Hos 12:3-5), Gideon (Judg 6:11-24), Zechariah the prophet, (Zech 3:1-6; 12:8) and Balaam (Num 22—24).

Question 4. Manoah seems to have struggled with an unwillingness to trust people. I believe he asked the Lord to send the angel back because he mistrusted his wife's report. When the angel of the Lord did appear to him, he plied the angel with questions and requests for information (vv. 11, 12, 17). He even tried to stall the angel so he would have more opportunity to question the angel (vv. 15-16). Finally, as is often the case with those caught in the web of doubt, Manoah was prepared to believe that only the worst results would come from their encounter with the angel (v. 22).

Question 5. The Lord placed on Samson the vows of a Nazirite. The word comes from the Hebrew word *nazir,* meaning to set apart. The details of the Nazirite vow are spelled out in detail in Numbers 6:1-21. Usually this vow was taken for a specific period of time, but God placed it upon Samson for life. The emphasis is usually on the negative restrictions of the vow, but more important to God was the positive consecration to the Lord (Num 6:8). The essence of the Nazirite vow was not negative abstinence but positive devotion to God.

Do not confuse the Nazirite vow with the New Testament reference to Jesus as a Nazirite or Nazarene. Those terms simply referred to Jesus' boyhood town of Nazareth. Jesus was from Nazareth, but he did not place himself under the Nazirite vow at any time.

Question 6. The emphasis should be focused not on what we don't do as Christians but instead on our positive consecration to Christ. Romans 12:1-2 urges us to reserve our lives for God alone. That means turning from sin and turning to God. The apostle Paul even refused things that were lawful so that he could concentrate more fully on following Christ (1 Cor 9:24-27; 10:23).

Question 7. The angel of the Lord is repeatedly referred to as "God" or "the Lord" by those who encounter him. This doesn't seem to be a case of mistaken identity either. Even the narrators of the passages refer to this being as deity. See, for example, Genesis 16:13 and Judges 6:11, 14, 16, 20.

Question 12. The word *angel* means "messenger." Even though the angel of the Lord is identified as deity, he functions as God's messenger. The term *angel* then describes his function rather than his nature.

Most evangelical Bible teachers believe that the angel of the Lord is a preincarnate appearance of Jesus Christ as God's messenger. He is certainly not the only angel to appear in the Old Testament, but he is always described in very distinctive terms as "the Lord." After Christ's incarnation, he never again appears as the angel of the Lord.

Study 4. Jesus and the Angels. Hebrews 1.

Purpose: To demonstrate the superiority of Jesus, God's Son, over the angels, God's servants.

Question 1. Encourage the group to think of a variety of answers, but be careful that the discussion on this question does not consume the entire study time. The purpose of the question is to focus attention on Jesus as God the Son and our Savior.

Question 2. At least seven declarations about Jesus appear in these verses: (1) He is the Father's appointed heir. All authority has been entrusted to Jesus (Mt 28:19). (2) He is the Creator (Col 1:16). (3) Jesus is the outshining of God's glory. When we look at Jesus, we see the invisible God made visible (Col 1:15). (4) He is the exact representation of God—not a godly reflection or a godlike being but God himself. (5) Jesus sustains the universe by his power. (6) He provided the means for us to be cleansed from sin by his death on the cross. (7) He is seated at the Father's right hand. The work of redemption is complete and Jesus now reigns over all as Lord.

The writer of Hebrews had one objective—to declare the uniqueness of Jesus the Son. No one and nothing in any realm of creation compares with Christ.

Question 3. The writer documents Jesus' superiority over the angels by referring to seven Old Testament quotations. The angels were created as "sons of God"—a wonderful position of glory. Jesus, however, existed forever in the relationship of Son to the Father. Jesus himself called God "the Father" or "*my* Father"—a claim the Jewish leaders correctly understood as a claim to equality with God (Jn 10:29-30, 33).

Question 4. Hebrews 1:8 is one of the clearest New Testament declarations of the deity of Jesus. In the quotation from Psalm 45:6-7, God the Father refers to Jesus the Son as God—"Your throne, O God, will last forever." The angels are God's servants; Jesus reigns as sovereign.

Question 5. The image of wind speaks of the angels' swiftness and their secretive work. We cannot see the wind, but we certainly feel its effects. (Compare the same image used of the Holy Spirit in John 3:8.) The image of flames of fire may convey the purity of these wonderful beings. These images may also indicate that the ministries of angels are changeable like the flickering of a flame or the shifting of a breeze. Jesus, in contrast, rules in a permanent position at the Father's right hand.

Question 7. The writer's emphasis is on the eternality and the unchangeableness of God. The created universe will perish (v. 7), but God remains.

Question 9. The fact that angels are inferior to Jesus should not discount their ministry to us. Just as they serve God (v. 7), they also are responsible to serve us under God's direction. Jesus is the focus of our worship and devotion as Christians, but we should not ignore the possibility of help from angels.

Question 10. Some Christians have been influenced by the New Age angel movement to believe that we should pray to or venerate angels in some way. The Scriptures are clear that we are never to worship angels. The pattern of prayer is to God the Father through God the Son in the power of God the Spirit. We are never instructed or encouraged to pray to angels or human beings.

Question 13. The answers to this question may stray too far into speculation. Try to anchor the expectations of the group to the biblical examples and declarations. An angel will not take that chemistry exam for you!

Study 5. Lower Than the Angels. Hebrews 2:5-18.

Purpose: To help us see the relationship between angels and human beings both now and in the future.

Question 2. God's original intention for humanity was that human beings should be sovereign over the earthly realm, subject to God alone. Adam and Eve were given a place of incredible honor and authority. This declaration of God's intention drawn from Psalm 8 is even more striking in the context of the full psalm. As the psalmist contemplates the enormous expanse of the star-studded sky, he is overwhelmed with the greatness of God, who designed and created such a universe—and he wonders why such a transcendent God would be concerned with such cosmic "specks" as human beings. The psalmist is astonished that the infinite God would lavish such attention and honor on puny humans.

Question 3. God's original purpose was delayed (not destroyed) by the intrusion of sin into the human realm. Sinful human beings can't even rule themselves properly, much less God's world.

Question 4. Jesus came to earth to redeem sinful human beings and to restore us to God's original place of honor. In order to do that, Jesus had to identify fully with us by becoming fully human himself. He was made "lower than the angels" in several ways. He had no visible glory during his earthly ministry (Jesus did not walk around with a halo), while the angels are magnificent in their glory. Jesus took on a human body with all of its limitations, while the angels are spirit beings who can move swiftly and who never grow tired.

Question 5. Jesus raises those who believe in him to the level of glory and honor that God intended human beings to inherit. Jesus was never morally imperfect but was made completely qualified ("perfect") to be our Representative and Redeemer through the experience of suffering. Jesus openly identifies us as brothers.

Question 6. Unless Jesus was fully human, he could not bear the penalty of human sin. As God, Jesus was able to pay an infinite price; as a human being, Jesus was able to pay the penalty of my sin. Belief in the full humanity of Jesus is as important to biblical faith as is a belief in the full deity of Jesus. If you remove either truth, you remove the possibility of genuine salvation.

Question 7. Satan's condemnation is already a certainty. The cross sealed Satan's destiny and secured Jesus' victory. Satan is still allowed, however, to tempt and to attack believers. We no longer have to submit to him, but he continues to set up schemes of attack against us.

Question 8. Death is the final great fear of human beings. Those who have not been cleansed by Christ fear the unknown; they fear the pain of death; they fear the separation from this world that death brings; and they fear the judgment that comes after death. In our culture, men and women will grasp at any shred of testimony about what follows death except the clear declarations of Scripture.

Question 9. The Bible never offers any provision for the salvation of sinful angels. Jesus did not come to earth as a God-angel but as the God-man. Angels who choose to follow Satan in his rebellion against God are sealed in their sinful condition forever.

Question 11. Human beings were the focus of God's original creation, we became the focus of Christ's redemption, and those who trust Christ will be the recipients of eternal glory. It is a far greater privilege to be a redeemed human being than a powerful angel!

Question 12. Christians will someday participate in the judgment of fallen angels. We will judge the very beings who oppress and oppose us now.

Study 6. Our Ancient Foe. Isaiah 14:3-15.

Purpose: To expose Satan as the believer's enemy and to discover Satan's plan of rebellion against God.

Question 2. Isaiah wrote long before the nation of Judah was taken captive by Babylon. He predicted the coming captivity and the ultimate release from Babylonian dominance. This taunt against the oppressive king would be taken up by God's people on the day of their release.

The rulers of the neo-Babylonian Empire from Nebuchadnezzar to Belshazzar were noted for their pride and arrogance before humanity and God. Each one suffered humiliation at God's hand.

Question 4. Not all Bible scholars agree that someone other than the earthly king of Babylon is in view in verses 12-15. If you think some in the group will challenge you on this point, you may want to consult a good commentary on Isaiah that will explain the various interpretations. The traditional interpretation (supported by many evangelical scholars and which I hold to) is that Isaiah looks beyond the proud earthly king and describes the real ruler of Babylon—Satan.

A similar interpretive issue is raised in Ezekiel 28, where Ezekiel speaks first to the "ruler" of Tyre and then beyond him to the evil "king" of Tyre, Satan. See Ezekiel 28:2, 11-19.

Question 5. The phrase "morning star" in verse 12 translated the Hebrew word *helel,* which means "shining one" or "day star." In the Vulgate and then through the Vulgate to the English Authorized (King James) Version it became Lucifer, a name often applied to Satan.

Lucifer became so proud of his beauty and position that he deceived himself into thinking that he could actually overthrow the sovereign Ruler of the universe. At that moment, Lucifer fell into moral sin. The "day star" became Satan, which means "the enemy" or "the adversary."

Question 9. God takes a consistently harsh position against pride throughout the Bible (Jer 49:16; 1 Pet 5:5-6) and specifically warns against it in church leaders (1 Tim 3:6).

Question 11. Satan's final expulsion from heaven (described in Revelation 12) seems to come at some future time just before Jesus' return in glory. Today Satan is allowed in heaven or even summoned to heaven to give an account of his actions to God (Job 1:6-7; 2:1). In that setting, "before our God" (Rev 12:10), Satan hurls accusations against us. The Lord Jesus is also in God's presence continually as our defender and intercessor (1 Jn 2:1). When not in heaven, Satan roams the earth seeking someone who is vulnerable to his attack.

Study 7. Dealing with Demons. Mark 5:1-20.

Purpose: To help us recognize both the reality of demons and the power of Christ alone to conquer them.

Question 3. The man was controlled by many demons (v. 9). They were able to control his speech and his actions and even to impart supernatural power to the man.

Question 4. Note verse 5 especially. Serving Satan is not fun. Also, the demons expected Jesus' judgment. They thought Jesus would send them to the Abyss (see Lk 8:31).

Question 5. Demons have remarkable spiritual insight! James says that the demons believe that God exists—they just don't have saving faith. The demons who controlled this man obviously knew Jesus and knew his true identity. Jesus usually told demons to be silent when they identified him publicly (see Mk 1:34). Jesus didn't want unsolicited testimony from demons even if they spoke the truth! In the situation in Mark 5, apparently only Jesus, his disciples and the tormented man were in Jesus' immediate presence, so Jesus did not command the silence of the demons.

Question 6. In our culture demonic activity will be displayed in very subtle, sophisticated ways. The highly educated person who denies God and God's presence in our world may be as influenced by demonic power as a shaman chanting magic incantations in a primitive culture.

Question 8. Responses to this question will be far-ranging. It is important to ground answers in the declarations of Scripture. It would be profitable, too, to warn those in the group from excessive interest in or involvement with demons. Satan and his hosts are defeated foes, but they are not to be taken lightly. We must have strong faith and spiritual maturity to face demons.

Question 9. My opinion is that a genuine believer who is indwelt by the Holy Spirit cannot at the same time be possessed by an evil spirit. Christians can, however, be demonized to varying degrees depending on their willingness to give Satan a foothold through disobedience or complacency.

Question 11. The synagogue ruler may have been more upset that Jesus healed a woman than that he broke the religious rules by doing it on the Sabbath.

Study 8. The Battle Against Us. Ephesians 6:10-20.

Purpose: To awaken us to the spiritual warfare raging around us and the resources that we have at our disposal.

Question 3. The phrases *rulers, authorities, powers of this dark world* and *spiritual forces of evil* convey the idea of a well-organized military campaign against us as believers. The image of fiery arrows and the command to stand our ground give us a glimpse of the offensive power thrown at us. This battle is not a mild skirmish but an intense barrage.

Question 6. A good Bible commentary that gives insight on the equipment of the Roman soldier will help you draw out the purpose of each piece of armor. One good resource is Craig Keener's *IVP Bible Background Commentary: New Testament* (Downers Grove, Ill.: InterVarsity Press, 1994), p. 554. Be sure to apply the description of each piece to its function in the *spiritual* battle.

Question 10. Prayer for each other points out the importance of soldiers standing together in battle formation. By himself a Roman soldier was vulnerable, but drawn together as a unit the army became almost invincible.

Study 9. Angels and Guidance. Acts 8:26-40; 10:1-48.

Purpose: To demonstrate how God may use angels to bring direction to his people and to compare that angelic work with the Holy Spirit's work of guidance.

Question 3. God has entrusted the proclamation of the gospel to human beings. One reason is that angels can never fully know what redemption is all about (1 Pet 1:12). Only men and women who have personally tasted the Lord's goodness can share the message of salvation with passion. In his own wise plan, God has chosen what appears to us to be a foolish method—proclamation—and weak vessels—us—to do the hardest task: telling the world about Christ (1 Cor 1:25, 27).

Question 4. The ministry of angels is primarily external, while the Spirit's ministry is internal. Angels focus on the physical realm as they guard our bodies and direct our pathway. The Spirit focuses on the spiritual realm as he guards our spirits and leads us in the right way. This comparison is expanded in C. Fred Dickason, *Angels: Elect and Evil* (Chicago: Moody, 1975), p. 101.

Question 5. The Lord used a prepared man (Philip) to lead another prepared man (the eunuch) to faith. We can be confident that, if we are willing to be used, God will lead us to people who are ready to listen to the message of salvation.

Question 8. Angels are a poor substitute for the Holy Spirit! God certainly *can* use angels to give us direction, but his preferred method of guidance is the voice of the Spirit within us.

Question 10. At times God may lead us into difficult situations to help us mature. Jesus was led by the Spirit into the wilderness to be tested by Satan (Mt 4:1). Objective confirmation of a decision prompted by the Lord may never come. In those situations we simply have to trust the One who sent us.

Question 11. The angel's messages were specific and were focused directly on the issues Joseph was facing. Furthermore, the angel's instructions were based on reasons that Joseph had no way of knowing personally. For example, the angel told him to flee to Egypt because Herod would try to kill Jesus. Herod's plan was a secret (except to God), but Herod's murderous reputation made it a believable possibility.

Study 10. Guarded by Angels. Acts 12:1-17.

Purpose: To explore what the Bible teaches about the protective care of angels over us.

Question 1. Responses to this question do not have to include the intervention of an angel; any story of protection will open the way into this text.

Question 2. King Herod in verse 1 is Herod Agrippa I. He was the grandson of Herod the Great, who had tried to murder the infant Jesus. Since A.D. 41, Herod Agrippa had ruled Judea and Jerusalem as a vassal king of Rome.

James (v. 2) was the first apostle to be martyred. This James was the brother of John and the son of Zebedee. He is to be distinguished from the James who later led the Jerusalem church and who (probably) wrote the New Testament book of James. The events in Acts 12 took place about ten years after Jesus' death and resurrection.

Question 5. God obviously could have supernaturally transported Peter out of prison. The personal angel was sent to bring a sense of comfort to Peter. The deliverance also became a dramatic demonstration of God's power through his holy angels.

Question 6. The only final answer to this question is that God is in control of life's situations, and God always does what is right. We may not understand his ways, but we can trust him and his love completely.

Question 7. You will get many opinions on this question. Try to balance an anticipation of God's intervention with a willingness to believe in God's goodness even if he doesn't intervene.

Question 8. The popular belief was that a person's "guardian angel" looked exactly like the person he protected. These Christians apparently believed that Peter had been executed and his angel had come to give them the news. It makes you wonder exactly what they had been praying for!

Question 10. The promise is to those who make the Lord their refuge. Satan tried to use this verse to tempt Jesus to jump from the highest point of the temple (see Mt 4:5-7). Jesus' response was that we are foolish to presume upon God's protection just because the devil dares us.

Question 11. Apparently, some of God's angels are assigned to stand prepared before the Father to respond instantly to his command for protection and care over these children. Jesus calls these particular angels "their [the children's] angels."

Question 13. We have only hints in Scripture about the protective care of angels, but the hints all point to the presence of guardian angels. In this area (as in so many other questions about angels) we cannot speak with absolute certainty. We can go as far as the Scriptures take us but no farther.

Study 11. Discerning the Spirits. 1 John 4:1-6.

Purpose: To help us evaluate spiritual experiences and angelic encounters according to God's truth.

Question 3. These Christians seem to be too willing to accept the testimony of anyone claiming to speak from God. John exhorts them to "test the spirits," meaning to put the claims of Christian teachers to the test. This theme is repeated in John's other letters (2 Jn 7-11; 3 Jn 4, 11). The believers at Berea were commended for laying the teaching of Paul alongside the measuring stick of God's Word to see if Paul's proclamation was true (Acts 17:11).

Question 5. One crucial "test" of a person who claims to speak from God is doctrine. The key doctrinal concept in John's mind is a person's view of Jesus Christ. Belief that "Jesus Christ has come in the flesh" involves the whole biblical teaching on who Jesus is. John's implication is that teachers who claim to expound God's truth must acknowledge that God the Son has come into space and time by means of the incarnation. If God has come to us in human flesh, we would expect his conception and birth to be miraculous (the virgin birth). We would expect his teaching to have the authority of God himself and to be accompanied by supernatural acts of power. We would expect his death to have an eternal purpose and we would expect the powerful testimony of the resurrection to be the climax of his ministry. For

John, the test question to ask any spiritual teacher is "What is your view of Jesus Christ?" If that teacher agrees with the Bible's declaration of who Jesus is, the teacher is from God. If the teacher denies any part of that pivotal truth, he or she is preaching a false Christ and should not be accepted.

Question 6. John's sharp contrast between truth and error is repeated in verses 4-6. "The one who is in the world" is a reference to Satan and to the worldview fostered by Satan that opposes Christ ("the spirit of the antichrist," v. 3). Christians can count on the fact that, when we align ourselves with the truth of God's Word, we will find ourselves in direct opposition to the popular worldview. The solution is not, however, to pull into evangelical fortresses but to stand courageously for God's truth in the middle of a culture dominated by the spirit of the antichrist.

Question 7. Other tests might be moral (Does the person's lifestyle conform to biblical standards of purity and Christlikeness?) or the love test (Does this teacher demonstrate genuine love for believers in his or her attitude and actions?).

Question 9. Someone will probably raise Jesus' injunction in Matthew 7:1 about judging others in response to this question. There is a difference, however, between self-righteous or hypocritical judgment (which Jesus condemns) and a proper judgment on truth and error. Jesus himself in the same context of Matthew 7 tells his followers to "watch out for false prophets" (7:15). The apostle Paul admonishes Christians to "test everything" (1 Thess 5:21). That judgment between truth and error and between good and evil is essential for our spiritual survival.

Question 11. Paul warns Christians to hold fast to the truth of the gospel even if they receive a different message from what appears to be a glorious angel. Even angelic messages are to be evaluated according to the clear declaration of God's truth in the Scriptures.

Study 12. God's Reapers. Matthew 13:24-50.

Purpose: To explore the role of angels in the end times and to evaluate our own preparation for Christ's return.

Question 1. The purpose of this study is not to debate specific schemes or outlines of end-times events. The focus of the group ought to be on the role of angels as agents of God's intervention in our world. Allow the members of your group to share their questions and possible answers but don't allow long discussion or debates to result. The goal of this question is to put the group in a future-looking frame of mind.

Question 3. In this parable, the angels are pictured as agents of divine judgment. They distinguish between those who are evil and the inheritors of the kingdom. They also escort those who are evil to the place of God's wrath.

Question 4. The distinction between "all who do evil" and "the sons of the kingdom" seems at first reading to be based on a person's works. Jesus, however, often used the actions of a person to describe the condition of the person's heart before God. Those who *do* evil are evil. They have refused to believe in Christ. The inheritors of the kingdom, on the other hand, do not enter God's kingdom because of their own merits but because of God's grace based upon the condition of genuine faith in his Son.

Depending on the makeup of your group you may want to follow up with the question "In which category would you place yourself and why?" This question provides an opportunity for a clear presentation of the gospel to your group. Be sure to emphasize that we do not become "good seed" simply by trying to do good deeds. We become good seed when our nature is changed by God. In Christ we are made God's new creation.

Question 7. The angels carry out the will of God, who knows our hearts and who judges rightly. Our human judgment is often faulty, but God's judgment never is (1 Sam 16:7). When the Father's kingdom is established, those who are evil are removed. Those who have been redeemed enter into the joy of the Father (see Rev 22:14-15).

Question 9. The most important response to this parable should be to be certain that we have put our faith in Christ alone for salvation. But the parable should also motivate us to action toward those around us who have not believed in Christ. God's judgment is coming and the destiny of those outside of Christ is certain.

Question 10. In this passage the angels are pictured as the rescuers of the righteous—the same role they played when they rescued Lot from Sodom (2 Pet 2:7-8; Gen 19).

Douglas Connelly is pastor of Cross Church and enjoys doing seminars on angels. Doug and his wife, Karen, live in Flushing, Michigan, with their three children, Kimberly, Kevin and Kyle. Doug is also the author of the LifeGuide® Bible Studies Meeting the Spirit, Daniel *and* John, *and the books* Angels Around Us *and* After Life.

What Should We Study Next?

A good place to start your study of Scripture would be with a book study. Many groups begin with a Gospel such as *Mark* (22 studies by Jim Hoover) or *John* (26 studies by Douglas Connelly). These guides are divided into two parts so that if 22 or 26 weeks seems like too much to do at once, the group can feel free to do half and take a break with another topic. Later you might want to come back to it. You might prefer to try a shorter letter. *Philippians* (9 studies by Donald Baker), *Ephesians* (13 studies by Andrew T. and Phyllis J. Le Peau) and *1 & 2 Timothy and Titus* (12 studies by Pete Sommer) are good options. If you want to vary your reading with an Old Testament book, consider *Ecclesiastes* (12 studies by Bill and Teresa Syrios) for a challenging and exciting study.

There are a number of interesting topical LifeGuide studies as well. Here are some options for filling three or four quarters of a year:

Basic Discipleship
Christian Beliefs, 12 studies by Stephen D. Eyre
Christian Character, 12 studies by Andrea Sterk & Peter Scazzero
Christian Disciplines, 12 studies by Andrea Sterk & Peter Scazzero
Evangelism, 12 studies by Rebecca Pippert & Ruth Siemens

Building Community
Christian Community, 12 studies by Rob Suggs
Fruit of the Spirit, 9 studies by Hazel Offner
Spiritual Gifts, 12 studies by Charles & Anne Hummel

Character Studies
New Testament Characters, 12 studies by Carolyn Nystrom
Old Testament Characters, 12 studies by Peter Scazzero
Old Testament Kings, 12 studies by Carolyn Nystrom
Women of the Old Testament, 12 studies by Gladys Hunt

The Trinity
Meeting God, 12 studies by J. I. Packer
Meeting Jesus, 13 studies by Leighton Ford
Meeting the Spirit, 12 studies by Douglas Connelly